All Things
Depending

All Things Depending

BRENDAN MULCAHY

THE CHOIR PRESS

First published in the United Kingdom in 2025 by
The Choir Press

ISBN 978-1-78963-549-2

For Catherine

Acknowledgements

Thanks to my wife Catherine, who is kindness personified.

Thanks to Jane and Rose, for their thoughtful pre-reading; Mary, for sharing smart ideas on licensed premises; Angela for her help with the cover image; and all the friends who have commented on poems at different stages in their making.

Thanks to Rachel, Adrian and Miles at The Choir Press for making the production of *All Things Depending* so easy and enjoyable.

Permission from Faber and Faber to use material from Samuel Beckett's *Malone Dies* in my poem *The Moment Comes When One Desists*.

Permission from Reuters to use the photograph accompanying the poem *Distrussed* on page 31.

The illustration to *Ahab* on page 16 is from a 1930 woodcut by Rockwell Kent.

The following poems appeared first in **Maura** (P2D Books Ltd, 2024): *Assimilating, The Day the War Started, Summerhill Interlude, Maura.*

Contents

1

Im Englischer Garten, München

Blue skies through a willow tree
your feet in fast-flowing water
thirty-three degrees and counting

Coalescence

Wimbledon Park, 2010 – present

On these courts,
in the compass of twelve years,
I have played the perfect match.
Served true down the T unreturned,
or out wide, to volley a lofted gimme
to the undefended corner opposite. Textbook.

I have kept points short, shunned the baseline,
called the shots with angles of irretrievability
and drop-shots weighted, placed to die
just so; with sleight-of-hand cross-court passes,
and, every so often, a ripsnorter
forehand down the middle flat and low.
All of these things have come to pass, performed
with feel and focus, tempered, in the zone.

A Fine Line

Lines on the passing of Wimbledon line judges

Tweedledum and Tweedledee
served the AELTC,
with only an occasional fail.
Unkindly terminated by email.

Way to go

In a Thalia bookshop in Heidelberg
you buy me a souvenir pencil,
complete with *radiergummi,* that
prevents it from slipping
through the rings on the spine of my notebook.

It's inscribed with a quotation
attributed to Kafka:
Wege entstehen dadurch, dass man sie geht.
Paths are made by walking.

Apocryphal, perhaps,
but we buy it anyway.
We're in holiday mode. All together now,
Wir fahr'n, fahr'n, fahr'n auf der Autobahn.

In the Casa del Libro, Los Arcos, Sevilla,
a different pencil legend reads,
Caminante, no hay camino:
se hace camino al andar.

Traveller, there is no path:
paths are made by walking.
Antonio Machado channelling Kafka,
or possibly Kafka channelling him.

Baubles
for a passing trade.
How easily we're seduced
by these mental tattoos.

Free, à Paris

Stipe says it's a metaphor
but everyone takes it literally.
You can see it in the video: he's
the shy guy who can't pull.
That's him in the corner
Losing his religion.

Paris, late spring.
A few steps down from Sacré Coeur's
brilliant alabaster basilica,
a guitar dude in plaid shirt and jeans
seduces a singalong throng into
losing their religion *ensemble*.

The metaphor and the irony are lost
here on the hill of Montmartre,
where the Communards took their final stand
for communism over communion.
But still each year, grey-haired laïcists
process to honour the gallant young

Chevalier de la Barre, dead
for disrespecting the bishop long ago.
Their numbers thin, they gather near
a statue sited stubbornly to confront
the fabulous church of the Sacred Heart –
removed by vengeful Vichy, mulishly restored.

Catholicism crowns the mount. Below,
the godless have the Square Louise Michel,
where the nonchalant young take the sun
and their good fortune for granted,
confessing a loss that leaves them
footloose, fuckable, free *à Paris*.

Gondolas

Venice does not need you, yet you come
to perch giddy, unconvinced,
on a scuffed red-leather throne
for eighty bucks and thirty mins a spin.

The gondoliers – hoop-shirted, lithe enchanters,
who carry off a boater better than an Eton toff –
look down on you, nonchalantly wielding their poles,
propelling incongruous, asymmetric shells across canals

of indeterminate chemical green.
Venice shows and tells. The merchants of Venice
never cut a deal. It's eighty bucks for five.
For two? The price is eighty bucks. You yield.

Duly spun and done, scales fallen from your eyes,
you're back at the bank, beneath the Bridge of Sighs.

St. Mark's Campanile, Venice

The city was not swayed by high-minded motives but by fear of being out
of pocket, the predatory commercial spirit of the fallen queen of the seas.
Thomas Mann: Death in Venice (1912)

To a pyramidal spire the Campanile soars up
above three hundred feet; in nineteen-o-two
its predecessor fell in just six minutes (one cat died).
Secure now, with elevator, and Angel Gabriel atop,
its square brick shaft dominates
Piazza San Marco, its Byzantine quadrupeds,
the lacework loggia of the Procuratie
and that delicate low-rise gilt basilica.

Why is it there? It was a watchtower once,
The master of the house, at the mouth of the Grand Canal.
Its bells rang out for half an hour
before an execution: Venetian power made manifest.
Its massiveness today offends the heart.
The ducat trumps the dreams of science and art.

Bloody L!

Your packing is meticulous, not so mine.
So, finding myself again – first time in Venice –
with insufficient underwear, my holiday
expenditure begins at Calvin Klein,
Calle del Teatro o de la Commedia.

At CK, they major on light, space
and shiny surfaces, chrome,
and *specialist fashion accessories*.
The presentation's fab but where's the stuff?
Okay, there's t-shirts, hoodies, jeans

but where are the foundation garments, *per favore*?
I spot them – they're side-on, not featured,
discreet little earners, not for display.
Dinky, translucent packaging reveals
Low-rise trunk 3-pack holiday pants.

It's as if they knew I was coming!
I take size M and cough up forty bucks
to the *soignée*, black-suited blonde
who doesn't ask, *is sir quite sure
that these are age-appropriate?*

Back at Rosa Salva, I try them on.
They're black, obligatory, but
the waistband choice is black, yellow or red.
I choose the red, of course, and ease them on.
You're all agog, you love my 'mini-pants'.

I swan about a bit, do mirrors, front and back.
They're swish, they're slick but will constrict
my manhood painfully, alas.
Living on the cusp from M to L,
I've goofed this time. I need the bloody L!

Your mission, should you choose to accept it:
returning barely-opened Calvin Kleins
(squeezed-in, if no longer pristine dink).
I'm up for it – no choice, really – and so
back to Calle Commedia I go.

No need for furtiveness. She's pleased to help,
finds me an L and pops it prettily
into their iconic bagadou.
I smile, urbane again,
Grazie, signora. Eccelente!

Welcome to our Kitchen

In Donegal, we learnt the Irish for 'kitchen'.
The café sign said C- I – S – T- I – N.
Savouring their soda bread and salmon,
we asked them to say it for us,

then couldn't remember it with confidence.
It's a 'k', like cuisine and küche.
It's not! She said, '*Ch*'! Didn't you hear her?
I kept out of it but fancied 'chisteen'.

We placed our souvenir plaque –
tasteful green uncials on a gold field –
above the Perrier mirror.
Kitchen life went on in its usual way,
John Coltrane and cassoulet.

Returning in time to the nub,
lenition intervened:
a weakening or softening of the sound,
by way of initial consonant mutation,
as after the possessive adjective 'ár'.

Our inscription did start with an 'ár'.
Aspirated thus, the C word
would indeed begin 'chist',
and we could finish off nicely
with a Manx 'een' tail.

Ár chisteen. Perfect.
Welcome to our kitchen:
Failte go ár gcistin.

Ah, now – that little preposition *go*
brings in eclipsis, *urú.*
And that
is a whole new poem.

Suckered by
The Quaker Graveyard in Nantucket

Take 1

Unconfident on a bike, I passed up the chance
to scuttle round Nantucket
on fat wheels with the rest,
got up in nautical shorts, picnic-ready.
It had been the same off the boat on Inishmaan,
an ocean away. Little could be achieved
on foot there too. But that was me.

And I was here now, so I took my book
to Prospect Hill, 'a non-sectarian,
not-for-profit cemetery association',
the one I supposed Lowell meant.
Peter Benchley had been recently interred
but I had passed on *Jaws* and didn't know.

It was making the best of a bad job.
No one spot in the grounds
felt more significant than any other.
I ate my lunch between unmarked Coffin
and Starbuck graves, then found
my Selected Lowell lacked
The Quaker Graveyard in Nantucket.

I may have read *For the Union Dead*
instead, with its 'graveyards
of the Grand Army of the Republic'.
Or maybe not. I read something,
then took pub comfort at Kitty Murtagh's,
or The Rose and Crown. Travelling alone, you do.

Take 2

A bumpy field at a busy cross-roads,
where Joy Street gives way to Hummock Pond Road,
Prospect Hill isn't much of a hill
and the graveyard isn't the graveyard sought.

I read Lowell's family elegy in situ, supposedly,
realising I've been tricked by a metaphor,
and all those Quaker mariners were drowned,
and most weren't even Quakers anyway.

Repairing to the Brotherhood of Thieves
for fine local Cisco beer, I weigh
accounts of pacifist Quaker whaling millionaires
against the fatal Hicksite schism that wiped them out.

Lowell's Quaker whalers were confected, balm
for private use. Nantucket now is all *Pequod*
and souvenir scrimshaw, two million bucks for
humdrum undistinguished real estate.
And Martha's Vineyard feels a world away.

Ahab

1
And thus,
Through the serene tranquillities of the tropical sea,
Among waves whose hand-clappings were
Suspended by exceeding rapture,
Moby-Dick moved on, still withholding from sight
The full terrors of his submerged trunk,
Entirely hiding
The wrenched hideousness of his jaw.

2
O whale!
The mad fiend himself is after you.
Blow your trump. Blister your lungs.
Ahab will dam off your blood.
All ye nations before my prow,
I bring the sun to ye.
I drive the sea.

3
Standing like an iron statue,
At his accustomed place,
Shaggy and black, with a stubborn gloom,
The old man's anvil purpose intensified.
His firm lips met like the lips of a vice.
For there is no folly of the beast
Of the earth which is not infinitely
Undone by the madness of men.

4

Look, ye Nantucketer –
Here in this hand, I hold his death –
Tempered in blood, and
Tempered by lightning are these barbs.
And I swear to temper them triply
In that hot place behind the fin
Where the white whale
Most feels his accursed life.

5

Ahab gazed beyond the whale's place
Towards the dim blue spaces
And wide, wooing voids to leeward.
In pursuit of those mysteries we dream of,
That either lead us on in barren mazes
Or midway leave us whelmed.

6

Ahab is forever Ahab, man.
This whole act's immutably decreed –
'Twas rehearsed by thee and me
A billion years before the ocean rolled.
Fool! I am the Fates' lieutenant,
Possessed by all the fallen angels.

7

Ahead through the horizontal vacancy,
A hump like a snow hill. *Thar she blows!*
It is Moby-Dick! The eternal sap
Runs up in Ahab's bones again.
I'll ten times girdle the unmeasured globe,
Yea, and dive straight through it,
But I'll slay him yet.

8

Diving beneath the settling ship,
The whale ran quivering along its keel.
I turn my body from the sun.
I feel my topmost greatness
Lies in my topmost grief.
Towards thee I roll,
Thou all-destroying but unconquering whale.

9

The harpoon was darted.
The stricken whale flew forward.
With igniting velocity
The line ran through the grooves, ran foul,
Caught Ahab round the neck and,
Voicelessly, as Turkish mutes bowstring their victim,
Shot him from the boat.

10

The drama's done.
But one
Did survive the wreck.

Floating on the margin of the ensuing scene,
Like another Ixion I did revolve.
Buoyed up by Queequeg's coffin
For almost one whole day and night,
I floated on a soft and dirge-like main.
Call me Ishmael.

The text is verbatim from Melville's great novel *Moby-Dick*.
The verse composition is mine.

2

"We hate poetry that has
a palpable design upon us"

Keats, 1818

Keats wasn't much of an activist,
Life being short and sad.
But he always got the poems done,
The Eve, the Urn and that.

Eight swans a-swimming

Eight swans swim into line on Plymouth Sound.
Behind, Drake's Island dereliction hides in murk.
Beyond, trees march on the Mount Edgcumbe skyline.

There is the wall that steadies me,
waiting for the swans to separate
while I point my new Olympus.
The grey on the later birds says cygnet,
and early morning grey predominates,
bar brownish furring on the shoreline rocks.
And just below the wall, observe
a small, adventitious orb of blue,
like a cartoon Covid icon to us now
(we can never not know what we know).

Somehow the snap became a photograph,
with lines to trace and claim intent.
And there is order, shaping, certainly.
But everything ultimately hinges
on those contingent, sequenced swans.

The Black Synagogue

Augsburg, August 2024

In the summer when Gaza was gutted,
Netanyahu still not removed,
we set foot in the synagogue at Augsburg,
on the unprepossessing Halderstrasse,
far from the city's hub of Renaissance wealth.

The only Bavarian synagogue
to survive the Nazis. Desecrated
on Kristallnacht, November '38,
fortuitously doused and spared
to protect the petrol station opposite.

We come through airport-style security,
keenly aware there's almost no-one here.
In German only, an austere Ukrainian
welcomes us, takes payment for entry
and I'm given a kippah to wear.

Leaving the bare vestibule, we climb
a dozen steps to the Black Synagogue,
which instantly astonishes:
all dark wood and objects of mystery.
The scale seems disproportionately vast.

Our eyes are drawn to a brilliant, raised menorah.
We struggle otherwise to decipher
the architecture and sacred paraphernalia.
You remark on the screens separating
male and female worshippers.

The building's style, we learn, is 1917 *art nouveau*,
its great 27-metre length and width
echoed in the height to the glittering dome.
Such confidence, these re-establishing
twentieth century Jews, banished but returned!

By April '42, all were gone. We pick
through puzzling artefacts in the museum,
Hebrew scripts that withhold their meanings,
but it's the photographs of family groups
in black and white that hold the heart.

In time the synagogue would be restored –
a few hundred came – before the miracle of Gorbachev
and *glasnost* brought refugees from the east
to swell the numbers to their former heights.
Fifteen hundred sang Hosanna here.

Elsewhere, millions came
from emptied shtetl steppes
to transform the land of promise, Israel.

Please Shout up into the Window

Epitaph for an Alfa Romeo

Down on the Thames the Battersea chimneys sunlit.
Here, between Suez Waste and Royal Mail,
a small tin bucket holds incongruous petunias.
Reception is an alcove,
where you're safe from HGVs
if you stand in.
Behind white-painted bars a notice reads,
PLEASE SHOUT UP INTO THE WINDOW.
A ripped sign warns against
'Threatening behav-'.
You're nervy in this rough male environment, come
from Wimbledon to Wandsworth Road to crush a car.

You really don't know how this place works. You guess
your car will be cannibalised for good bits,
then crushed, so many miles clocked, bought from new.
But you've rejected the nostalgic route – it's okay –
so it's a sweet shock when you hear,
Must be 'eart-breakin' to scrap a lovely motor like tha'.
'ow much they give you?

And suddenly it's clear
that everyone conducts themselves with courtesy and charm.
No hint of meanness. No horses frightened.
Renata from the office, leaning though the window
below the bars, is an absolute pro,
smiles enough, sends up *our lovely council*.
She hands me my Certificate of Destruction,
and shows me how to claim the Mayor's begrudging shilling.

Souvenir

Panic Wednesday at big Sainsbury's,
Colliers Wood, 25th March 2020:
'oldsters only' allocated
the 7 to 8 a.m. slot.
Your caring, sharing caterers showing they care.

At ten to eight,
How old are you? rings out
accusingly around the lot,
where flip-flopped, double-
waggoned couples bristle.

Opting smartly for a basket
(our toilet roll supply was up to scratch),
I shot straight to the front of the queue
and in. Bread and fruit I guess I got,

then landed in a throng on
the medicine aisle, where a hassled
stacker thrust two packs
of Paracetamol into my hands.

Arriving home unscathed,
your gratitude
seemed disproportionate.

The packs remain unopened.
Expiry January '22.

Yachts not to like

When I visualise a yacht
I see clean lines,
a varnished hull, white sails,
a mainmast and a jib. *Yachting.*

From the Dutch *jaght*(schip),
for 'chasing' in Collins, 'hunting' (OED);
'a light, fast sailing ship', the emphasis
on sleekness and speed.

Today, Google generates
shots of metal-clad monsters –
yours for half a billion –
oligarchs' floating dachas overblown;

tax-efficient fortresses
with the grace and allure
of a Zumwalt-class
stealth destroyer.

Plume-plucked Richard

I next ran into Johnson in July,
moving in the crowds at the Globe.
In company, not drawing attention, suited
but tieless, hair trim, in for
The Life and Death of King Richard the Second .

You knew that this King's Scholar knew the score –
the power-play, indecision, frittering, favourites – foresaw
the *plume-plucked* monarch's desperate cri de coeur:
Let us sit upon the ground
And tell sad stories of the death of kings.

You knew he knew it well: a Falstaffian
pole-dancing mayor, who'd signally
failed to declare an interest, and
spaffed forty million of the people's pounds
on a chimerical garden bridge.

Time was running out at City Hall.
With Cameron back at No 10
(but hamstrung by his craven guarantee),
what thoughts were racing through the mind
of the would-be world-king, zip-wire mayor?

It was time to invent those columns yea and nay,
for, truth to tell, Johnson didn't care,
and Brexit was the merest bagatelle.

I come to thee
From plume-plucked Richard, who with willing soul
. . . his high sceptre yields.
Richard II, Act 4 Scene 1

Distrussed

Liz Truss resigns as Prime Minister, October 2022

Hot on the heels of
Johnson citing Cincinnatus,
in the season of Downing Street clear-outs,
the most improbable Prime Minister takes leave
without apology.

The rogue Boris had discharged himself before a claque
of appreciative blondes and blue-suits; but Truss is
bounced back on her tod to her sparse family flock.
They say, *Home is the place where, when you
 have to go there, They have to take you in.*

The railing carries the eye from left to right,
from a rearing jenga cobra to an ill-assorted trio,
sunlit after autumn rain.
Dad is buttoned-up, and out of place,
unsure how to look or be. Big girl
smiles conspiratorially at Mum, as
little sis peeps out in her New Look best.

Accoutred all in forest green,
Truss performs her practised walk,
that hemline on the calf unflattering,
her soles still advertising Mil.

Ringfencing Richard

The Globe Theatre cast a female, non-disabled
Richard III in their summer programme, 2024.

The lady's not offended in the least
to learn that Michelle Terry plays the lead.
Born on the same date Richard himself expired,
she claims affinity. Like him, she suffers
spinal curvature, but she insists that
people with different disabilities
have different lived experiences.
Richard is not a disabled part per se.

Mat Fraser, though, is *done with the pretenders.*
Born with undeveloped arms,
he played Richard to acclaim with Hull Truck.
Now he's boycotting the Globe.
Take this part away from us -
it's like we're being excluded from the stage.

So, should we ring-fence *Richard*, see it as
a part apart, quite unlike other parts?
Perhaps. But *Crook-back* is a visual metaphor:
Rudely stamped, I am a villain.

And yes, I know the economics, Mat:
90% of actors do get screwed.
But protectionism cuts both ways.
Hem yourself in and other doors will close.

The very best of *play* is still a version,
a fair stab at authenticity.
It's not the same as being something else.
All artists have the right
to play all parts, they say at the Globe.
Seems fair to me. Well, fair enough.

.

3

Mixed Doubles

It doesn't work, you say.
I say okay, end of story.
A sad denouement, even so.

I Feel Fine

50,000 cram Fifth Avenue.
Crazed electrons spark.
The Beatles nod the Supremes
to their penthouse at the Plaza Hotel.
First time in New York,
nonchalant, top of the charts.

Chaperoned, the girls arrive –
chic in suits and gloves, fur wraps,
to find the four boys sprawled in jeans,
off their heads in a marijuana haze.

Impasse.

How can the lovable Moptops be such doped-out slobs,
the Motown soul sisters such prissy squares?

David Niven's archetypal English gent
and Bessie Smith's
louche empress of the blues
have much to answer for.
So hard for each to see the others as they are.

Insolent Sixties England pitches
rock 'n roll right back at the States,
shocking upwardly-mobile black Detroit
to the roots of its Silvikrined hair.

Stoppage and Flow

High up in the Festival Hall
on a windswept March night,
in the sound-proof Voice Box,
in the last year of the millennium,
Brendan Kennelly enfolds his hearers in a watery tale.

He has lived through a quadruple heart by-pass
and shares with us his new work,
The Man Made of Rain –
visions from the interstice
between life and death.
Let me happen to you, said the man.

His pouring visitant triggers
memories of a murder in a field near Listowel,
a turfy-lipped molester in the west of long ago,
a Dublin gangster living with a hammer,
and hapless Dulcet Scruffy on his London building site.

The time he was clocked on O'Connell Bridge
for giving Cromwell right of reply,
landing in the hard and damp,
his shoulder crashing a stanchion.
The man of rain smiles his smile of mercy.

Shy behind metal specs, our survivor smiles too –
Bones and stories. No coddin' –
breathes shallowly, and, resuming, is
ambushed by a clamant mobile phone, that
misses the moment and rings and rings.

He waits, regathers us. *There is*
a now that cannot be grasped, he says.
And we, who have never been to Listowel, concur.

Ashes to Ashes

An amateur historian
questions the provenance
of the Hardy Ash, that crashed
in Old St. Pancras churchyard
in December twenty twenty-two.

Ashes are the opportunists
of the arboreal world, they say;
good for a few hundred years
with luck, becoming
lightning rods for the historical imagination.

Legend has it Hardy helped
to stack the stones to
stay that mighty ash,
where the Shelleys had tiptoed
permissively, and later
Mary Wollstonecraft would lie.

We need that tree to have
predated Hardy,
witnessing sunlit
Shelley trysts, providing
shade for Mary's long lying in.

A post-war upstart ash,
toppling after sixty years,
just replicates our own
three-score something stint.
We need an ash that bookends us,
that tells us life goes on.

The Moment Comes When One Desists

On receiving a copy of Malone Dies, the day of my retirement from teaching. The phrases are Beckett's, reassembled from unrelated places in the novel.

He attended his classes.
This exercise-book is my life.
Space hemmed him in on every side
and held him in its toils.
Harassed mobs scurrying from cradle to grave
to get to the right place at the right time.
And without exactly building castles in Spain, for that.

The moment comes when one desists.
I shall play a great part of the time from now on,
the greater part if I can.
Whole evenings of prestidigitation and ventriloquism
in the moonlight on the terrace.
The yesses, noes, mores and enoughs that keep love alive.

I must say there is something very attractive about such a
prospect.
A taper is all one needs to live in strangeness,
if it fruitfully burns.
My sliver of sky is silvery with it yet.

Hat-trickery

Grave-spotting throws up
Stephen, Levy and Marx:
Woolf-father, Small-Islander
and Karl himself, manifest
in a half-acre in Highgate East

In Cheshire once, my landlord bet
(no stake) I couldn't land
three consecutive ten-foot putts
in his exec putting machine. I did.
He raised the rent.

Au Cimetière de Levallois-Perret,
lie Ravel, Michel and Eiffel;
Maurice, Louise et Gustave le Magnifique,
flung together by fate,
the blueprint for a limerick.

More Roads Not Taken

One should be satisfied with what works moderately well.
Voltaire: Candide

We didn't fly to Le Touquet
with Andrew and Belinda.
He'd got his hours in and talked it up –
Oxonian lawyer, kept wicket –
but would you feel safe in one of those?
Not this Irish airman.

Meeting George and Martha
in the bar at Del Mar,
we declined their invitation to the Rancho Santa Fe.
We're friendly and uncomplicated. Okay,
but their way with food betrayed
an attitude you really couldn't trust.
And who would ever find us way out there?

We bought that Chicago guidebook nine years ago now.
The Memphis / New Orleans drive remains undriven.
Je ne m'informe jamais de ce qu'on fait à Constantinople.[1]
The world will always be too much with us.

---

[1] *I'm not concerned about what goes on in Constantinople.*

Where do they keep the lions?

a child asks, in the Greek amphitheatre at Taormina

The lions on their motor bikes
come roaring through the streets
on Hondas and Ducatis
to perform outlandish feats.

The tenors and sopranos
are gargling pre-show:
the lions stow their crash-hats
in their lockers down below.

The make-believe of *La Bohème*
detains the crowd a trice,
whilst teeth are sharpened, manes are combed;
what's coming isn't nice.

They enter *sotto voce* –
it wouldn't do to growl –
and mingle with school parties,
cheek by jowl.

The kids find them exotic.
They soon command the floor:
you'd swap the lady with the cough
for a splash of blood and gore.

Arrrrr . . . . . arrrrrrrgh! soon resonates.
They're warming to their task.
The nibbling and the gnawing next –
nobody has to ask.

Her tiny hand is frozen
. . . but her calf is dripping blood.
It starts with a few droplets
but it soon becomes a flood.

Ahem, ahem! Poor *La Bohème*
approaches her demise.
Behold her mauled and mangled.
Hear the little children's cries.
With helmets on, the lions leave
as *pauvre Mimi* dies.

The Replacement

She takes the replacement
to lunch at the Rising Sun:
the place for steak,
fine reds and a line of pumps
dispensing local ale.

The blue-eyed one carelessly lost,
the newbie has to pass the social test.

She plumps for a favoured corner seat.
He's on a stool

with an outsize menu, feet
vexed by bumpy cobbles;
a new shirt constricts his neck.

Sheepishly, he admits
he is teetotal,
and a vegetarian.

She's thunderstruck.
Why do they always miss the vital stuff?

The kitchen knocks together soup
and cheese for him. He asks for
a glass of lemon and lime.

With the staff handbook for afters,
the veil of mercy
must be drawn on this charade.

Six months on, he's up before the beak,
explaining that red ink
stifles his pupils' creativity.
He's told to mark his 'bloody books',
sees the year out, and
qualifies for redundancy.

4

Going Far

10 out of 10 in soft crayon.
My Irish had been on the mark at six.
Can you see the *coinin bán* in the *sneachta?*
There he is!
An buachaill leis na súile gorma will go far.
And lose his Irish in the going.

Assimilating

In England there'd been a war.
You had to learn to be a Spitfire,
wings out, a-a-ah-ing down the yard.
You had to take your shots,
bagsy and have dibs. Whatever.
Anthony Pearce drew falling
cable cars. You couldn't draw.
And, reading aloud in class, you learnt that
Briton and Brighton weren't the same.

You absorbed and were absorbed,
Quite easily it would seem.
Doing well, not top but close, and no
friendship hang-ups. Girls would be harder.
We were poor but we subscribed
and the future would take care of itself.

Martin

Martin sat on my office desk all day,
uncommented on, turfed out
unceremoniously from his car-door perch
as I scrambled for a train at Wimbledon.
You'd driven off, and there he was in the road.
What's a man to do?

A six-inch cuddly tiger on my desk,
musing on defenestration.

Cheffy buys an *Up!*
Martin's wedged in another car door.
The perch is shallower, he's vulnerable.
And duly out he goes, unnoticed this time,
in our home car park.
Returning, you found him face down in the asphalt,
but unfazed.
Two lives gone, Tiger Pet:
prends soin de toi!

Wetherby Services, heading North, M1.
We break for lunch, making good time.
Costa and a sandwich, 'sokay.

'Someone's left their rubbish on your roof!'
It's a shiny white *Up!* And something
is spoiling the look.

'It's Martin!' Face down again
but unperturbed.

Joy-bringer, talisman of the roads, desist!
It's the Valerie* in you, forever scenting freedom.
But we require your cheery presence yet
for years and years and years.

---

*My free-spirited sister, from whom we inherited Martin

Pat and Val

I find him heading an outstanding school
in a snug Cornish town, a lifetime
away from the backwoods of Burnt Oak.
Who back then would have envisaged 'Dr Pat',
the chip on his shoulder practically worn away?

Val left us back in 2012,
on a warm night in Southend General.
She didn't have your hang-ups, Pat –
she had her own, and some –
but PhDs were strictly for the birds.

Hard to think that you two
shared a desk at school. But you did.
Shuffled by fate together for a trice.
But you remember her with tenderness
forty aspirational years along.

Eleven plus failures both.
It burnt your soul like acid.
She accepted it as just the way things are.
Your way was perfectionism, grit.
She tackled every hurdle ill-equipped.

Grammar School was an unearned cruise
for some. Excluded, you made damn sure
you were better than the rest. Angelic
in her bottle-green skull-cap (two clips),
Val didn't even know it was a race.

O Levels, A Levels cashed in,
you were off on the accolade trail.
And once you'd scored the big one
(dissertating on … *what was it, Pat?*)
'Doc' was on your door forever more.

The Day the War Started

for Maura and Stephen

The story goes: it's the third of September
and no such undertaking has been received.

In Cork they await the *Innisfallen's*
return from Fishguard in the land of dreams.
They're fog-bound and the ship is overdue.
Crowds gather on St. Patrick's Street.
The *Lusitania* bubbles up in minds and mouths,
lost off the Old Head of Kinsale,
… and the *Titanic* had last been seen at Cobh.

I see you near the Savoy, after Mass at St. Mary's.
You're 23. He's 24. What fateful friction joins you?
He surely raises his hat
to the pretty girl from the north side.
And you find yourself listening; he speaks softly.
With no phone numbers to swap,
the fascination has to hold.
Did he meet you next under Mangan's clock,
the boat back and the world in shock?

Summerhill Interlude

The Move
Why did we move to Summerhill?
We were suddenly just there,
the Highcliffe dream
in smithereens.

Elizabeth Bowen's
snuggle of Gothic villas –
seen from an arriving packet-boat –
had long lost its cosy cachet.

Untrained
Home now was a shabby 1830s
end terrace. Untrained hydrangea
took light from the basement kitchen;
fuchsia in the garden behind grew

over the wall, where milk
was delivered from a churn at the side gate.
War of Independence bullet holes
scarred the dingy plasterwork.

Unexplained
Who owned it? Not us.
Granny was twenty-five years a widow,
slowly going down with the house.
A couple rented on the ground-floor.

The three of us camped in a single bedroom,
one floor up; a rusty, cold-water bathroom
adjoined. Dad was in England, I learnt.
At six you just find out.

Three Windows Wide
I don't remember being unhappy.
The first floor sitting room was fabulous –
three windows wide and gazing out
over the Lee and its boats and its trains.

An unplayed piano, with Jim and Biddy's
wedding photos, faced the open fire.
A lengthways table held a silent wireless,
in the days before rock and roll.

Dinkys

I'm on the floor, with a pile of cigarette packs,
building. Uncle Bernie made me
Brendan's Garage to store my Dinkys,
a chunky blue Rover my favourite.

Auntie Rita bought me a rubber football –
I thought it was fruit when she said, *guess*.
And I came by a hurley somehow,
but somehow I never hurled.

Temperament

Trying on a gas mask, smashing a rosary
in a temper on the deal table,
where my sister staged Whip-Crack-Away
when we were taken to *Calamity Jane*.

Going sweet on a girl at No. 3,
waiting for her by the post-box.
The *Mr What* Grand National draw –
I listen long in vain for *Sam Brownthorn*.

Catch!
Mum rowing with Mr Joyce next door and crying.
She seems to cry a lot, but sneaks us on a train
for the beach, distilling magic from duress.
I wear bright red trunks.

Dad's back from England saying, *D'you follow?*
He explains cricket. Unaccountably,
I catch the ball and live on the glory
for days. He slips away again.

Way Out
School said I was *an excellent pupil.*
I had a friend and watched out
for the rough-and-ready army kids.
I was learning to get by.

Then Cork was done, and we were off.
That was fine by me. My roots were shallow.
The boat leaves Penrose Quay on a Friday night
and life resumes next week in Harrow.

Maura

It was never fair on you.
Loss piled on loss, and you had to leave
the house on Highfield Lawn –
the kiddies gorgeous in their coats and shoes.
Always scrabbling after that.

Never cracked England but stuck it out.
Unnerved, keeping on
when hope was gone. You were
good around the nuns and lost
him every Friday to the Queen's.

No cute hoor you; the wans from
the West got houses to your awful flat.
The streets *were* paved with gold.
Labourers bought lorries: pen-pushing cut no ice.
Gentle, distressed, you just got by.

Back

We gotta get out of this place.
The Animals

The bridge, Wealdstone – Harrow.
The station, Harrow and Wealdstone,
where the almighty crash took place in '52.
The Railway pub, where they discovered The Who.
On the downslope the social club
where the Pogues played on the up.
The garage on the corner, with the phone box,
when we didn't have a phone.
Today, the colossal Harrow Central Mosque
commands that view on Station Road.

The Samaritans are at 44 now,
the yellow-brick where we spent the Sixties.
I'm let in for a look, though clearly suspect –
they've seen it all.
We lived upstairs in the middle flat.
They show us round the Westlake place
downstairs, where Vera tried to take her life,
and Kieran almost took us out
with a Friday night chip-pan fire.
A coarse charcoal carpet
runs throughout. The paper's stained.
No love lost, no reason to come back.

Marie, Marie, hold on tight!

You are marooned 600 metres from home. Still clear-eyed and blonde, slender vestige of a 30s Berlin gym display. Your companion struggles to hold you upright now. *Are you okay? No, her* legs *have gone. I would have called an Uber but I couldn't let her go.* You'd circled the park and run out of puff on the home stretch. You can't lean on your stick, so we lend you an arm apiece and off we go. *It's Number 9,* you say. We gauge the pace and the footfalls, talking about tennis. *She was a great athlete, you know. A cyclist and a tennis player. Never missed Wimbledon.* Now here you are stalled, only yards from the grounds. You can't recall a favourite player: *Federer? ... Becker? ... Graf?* Your Mitteleuropean friend sticks up for Djokovic. *So unfair. He's done great things for his country.* We make a right turn. The road is uphill now. You feel you are falling but we hold you tight until we reach the black iron gates of Number 9, a towering cypress and a fountain in the grounds. We ride three floors up in the lift, and perch you on the first of two ivory sofas. Your feet skim the deep-pile carpet.